D0518135

What Is Money?

Veronica Lane Books

What
Is
Money?

By Etan Boritzer   Illustrated by Jennifer West

V_L_B *Veronica Lane Books*

www.veronicalanebooks.com email: books@veronicalanebooks.com
2554 Lincoln Blvd. Ste 142
Los Angeles, CA 90291 USA
Tel/Fax: (800) 651-1001

Library of Congress Cataloging-In-Publication Data
    Boritzer, Etan, 1950-
    What is Money / by Etan Boritzer
    Illustrated by Jennifer West — 1st Edition
    p.   cm.

SUMMARY: Presents childrens with an understanding of financial responsibility and discusses the intrinsic nature of money, its history and diverse uses.

Audience: Grades K - 6

ISBN 0976274329 (Hardbound)
ISBN 0976274337 (Paperback)

The Library of Congress No. 2005908101

1. Children Finances, Juvenile Lit. [Finances]
2. Money, Juvenile Lit.

332.1'0973

This publication was supported in partnership with THE ART FUND CORPORATION.
www.theartfundcorporation.com

...to the children
of the world...

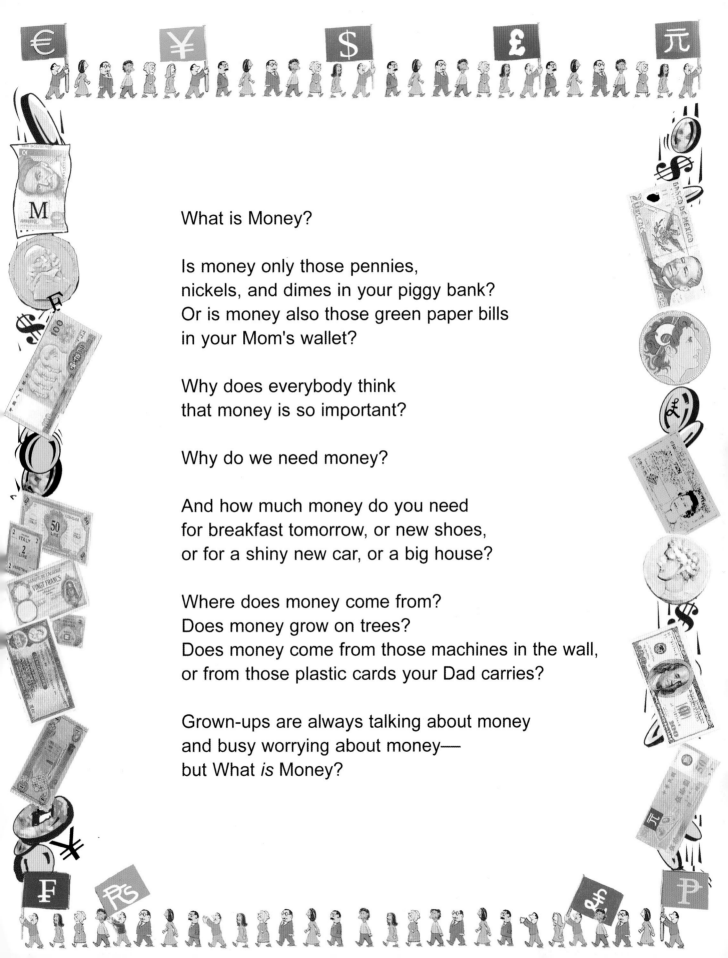

What is Money?

Is money only those pennies,
nickels, and dimes in your piggy bank?
Or is money also those green paper bills
in your Mom's wallet?

Why does everybody think
that money is so important?

Why do we need money?

And how much money do you need
for breakfast tomorrow, or new shoes,
or for a shiny new car, or a big house?

Where does money come from?
Does money grow on trees?
Does money come from those machines in the wall,
or from those plastic cards your Dad carries?

Grown-ups are always talking about money
and busy worrying about money—
but What *is* Money?

What is Money?

We can buy all kinds of stuff with money
but is there stuff we *can't* buy with money?
What can't we buy with money?

I can buy an ice cream
but can I buy an iceberg?
I can buy a pillow
but can I buy a cloud?
I can buy a puppy
but can I buy a puppy's love?

Is there somebody who can tell me
what to buy and what not to buy?

What if there was no money
and we couldn't buy *anything*?
How could we get the stuff we need—
like food and clothing and a house?

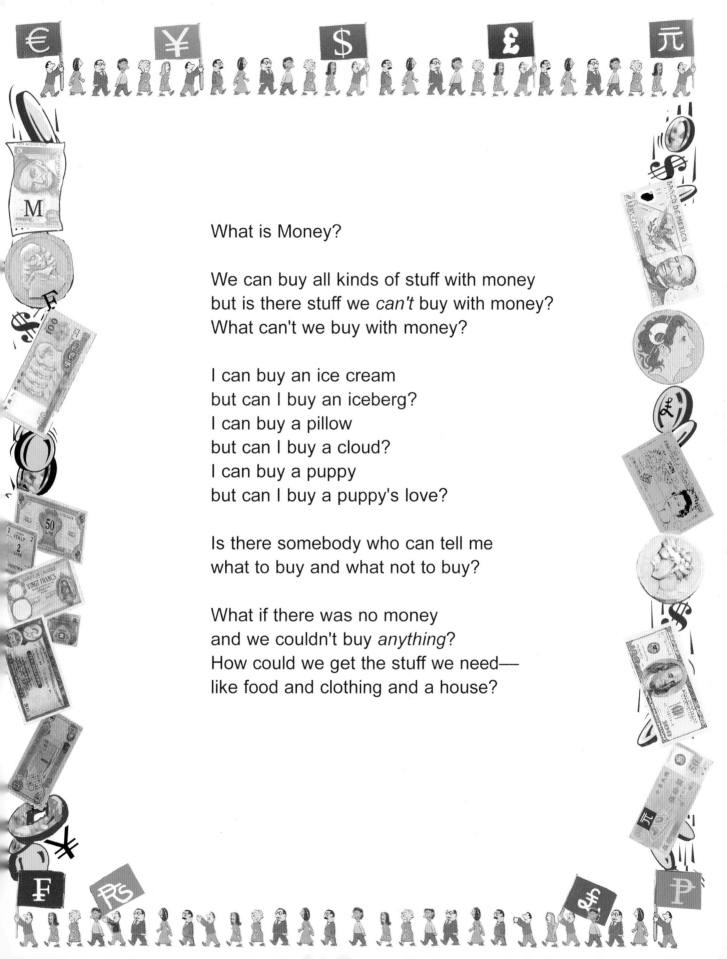

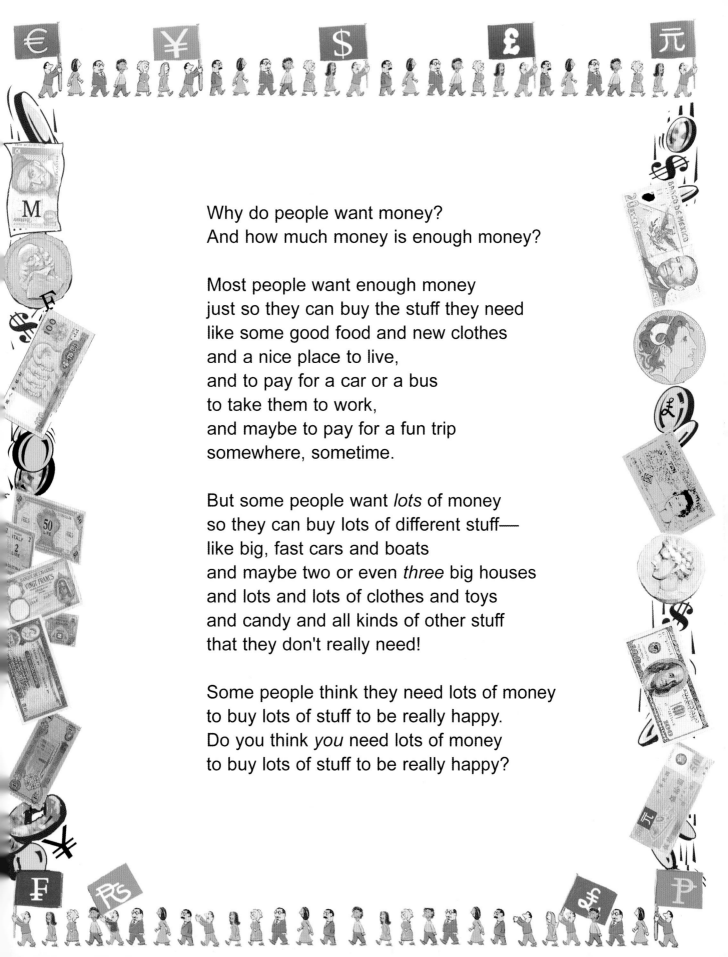

Why do people want money?
And how much money is enough money?

Most people want enough money
just so they can buy the stuff they need
like some good food and new clothes
and a nice place to live,
and to pay for a car or a bus
to take them to work,
and maybe to pay for a fun trip
somewhere, sometime.

But some people want *lots* of money
so they can buy lots of different stuff—
like big, fast cars and boats
and maybe two or even *three* big houses
and lots and lots of clothes and toys
and candy and all kinds of other stuff
that they don't really need!

Some people think they need lots of money
to buy lots of stuff to be really happy.
Do you think *you* need lots of money
to buy lots of stuff to be really happy?

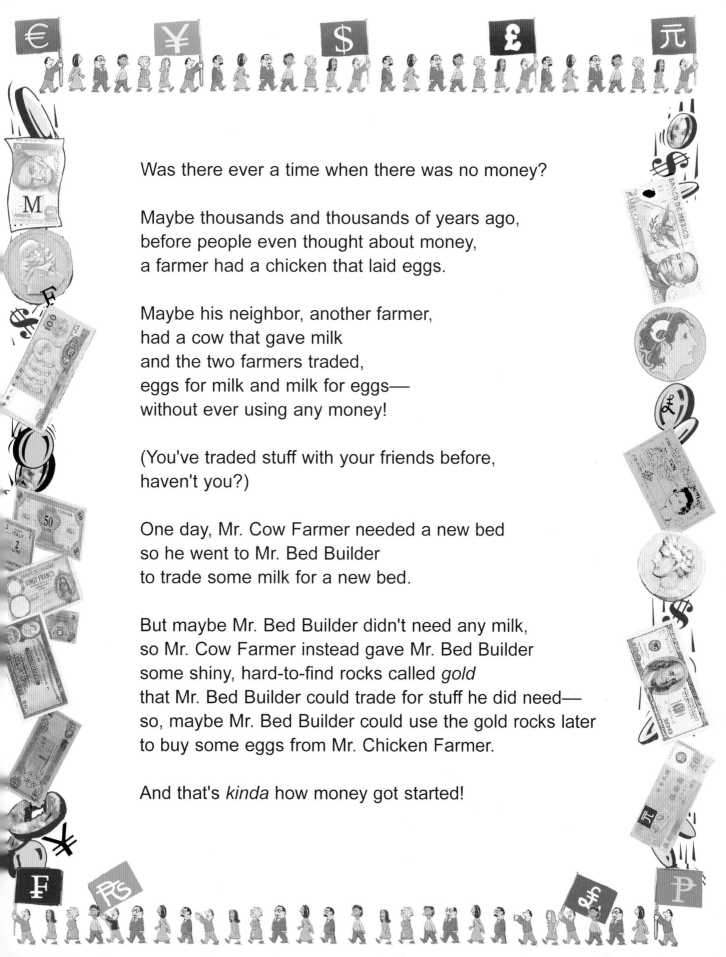

Was there ever a time when there was no money?

Maybe thousands and thousands of years ago,
before people even thought about money,
a farmer had a chicken that laid eggs.

Maybe his neighbor, another farmer,
had a cow that gave milk
and the two farmers traded,
eggs for milk and milk for eggs—
without ever using any money!

(You've traded stuff with your friends before,
haven't you?)

One day, Mr. Cow Farmer needed a new bed
so he went to Mr. Bed Builder
to trade some milk for a new bed.

But maybe Mr. Bed Builder didn't need any milk,
so Mr. Cow Farmer instead gave Mr. Bed Builder
some shiny, hard-to-find rocks called *gold*
that Mr. Bed Builder could trade for stuff he did need—
so, maybe Mr. Bed Builder could use the gold rocks later
to buy some eggs from Mr. Chicken Farmer.

And that's *kinda* how money got started!

But we don't use gold rocks for money anymore—
so, what happened to all those gold rocks?

The gold rocks are still found today
in some deep caves in the earth.
But after a while it became too much trouble
to carry all those gold rocks around,
especially if you wanted to buy big stuff
like a whale or an airplane or a really tall building!

So then, somebody figured out
that you could melt the gold rocks into coins
by putting the gold rocks over a very hot fire.
And that's how gold coins got started.

But then after another while,
it became too much trouble
to carry all those gold coins around,
especially if you wanted to buy
really, really big stuff like an island
or a mountain or a city.

So later somebody thought up paper money
(called *paper bills*)
and that's what we use today—
like maybe one old gold coin is worth
lots of paper bills now,
but I don't really know how many, do you?

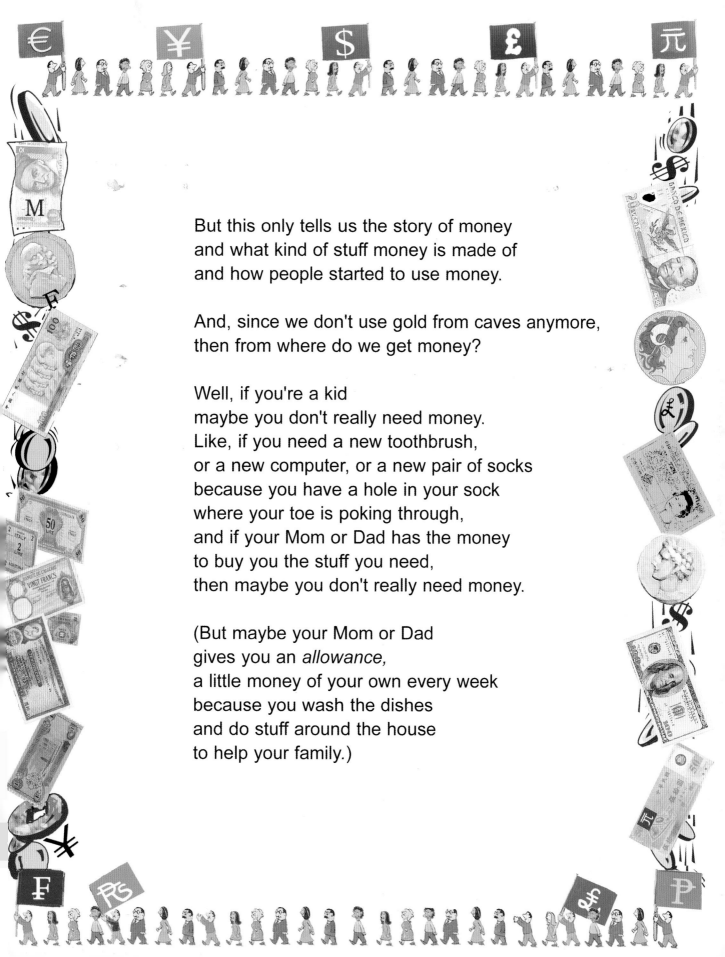

But this only tells us the story of money
and what kind of stuff money is made of
and how people started to use money.

And, since we don't use gold from caves anymore,
then from where do we get money?

Well, if you're a kid
maybe you don't really need money.
Like, if you need a new toothbrush,
or a new computer, or a new pair of socks
because you have a hole in your sock
where your toe is poking through,
and if your Mom or Dad has the money
to buy you the stuff you need,
then maybe you don't really need money.

(But maybe your Mom or Dad
gives you an *allowance,*
a little money of your own every week
because you wash the dishes
and do stuff around the house
to help your family.)

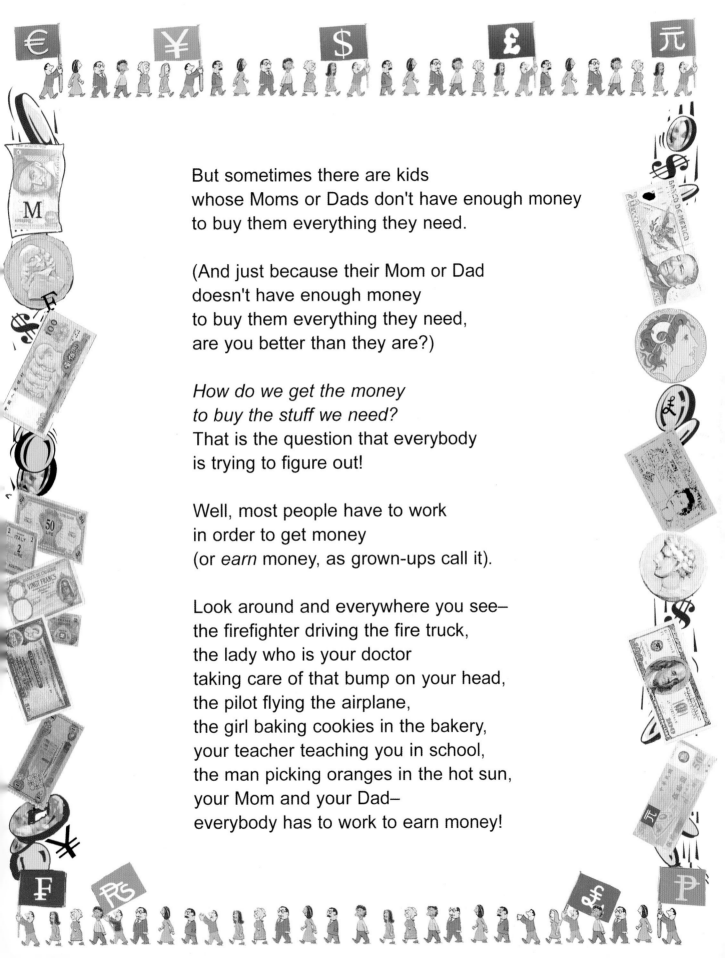

But sometimes there are kids
whose Moms or Dads don't have enough money
to buy them everything they need.

(And just because their Mom or Dad
doesn't have enough money
to buy them everything they need,
are you better than they are?)

How do we get the money
to buy the stuff we need?
That is the question that everybody
is trying to figure out!

Well, most people have to work
in order to get money
(or *earn* money, as grown-ups call it).

Look around and everywhere you see–
the firefighter driving the fire truck,
the lady who is your doctor
taking care of that bump on your head,
the pilot flying the airplane,
the girl baking cookies in the bakery,
your teacher teaching you in school,
the man picking oranges in the hot sun,
your Mom and your Dad–
everybody has to work to earn money!

When people work,
they get paid money for their work.
But who pays all these people when they work?

Most of the time, the person who pays the money
to the person who works is called the boss
or the manager or the *President of the Company*
(or even *The Big Cheese,* but don't ask me why).

The person who works for the boss
is called the worker or the *employee*.

The boss can be a woman or a man
or even another kid, if you work for him or her.
And the boss is the person who pays the workers.

Usually, the boss is the person
who works the hardest,
or is the smartest, or both!
And he or she earns the most money!

But who pays the boss?
The boss is paid by the *customer*.
A customer is the person who pays
for something the boss does or makes.

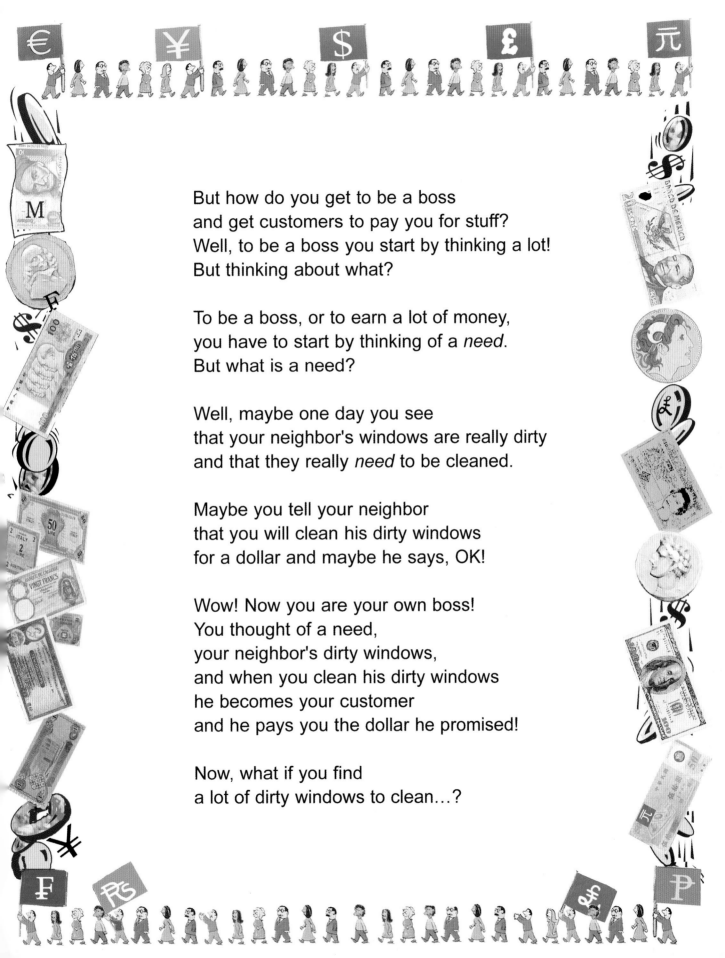

But how do you get to be a boss
and get customers to pay you for stuff?
Well, to be a boss you start by thinking a lot!
But thinking about what?

To be a boss, or to earn a lot of money,
you have to start by thinking of a *need*.
But what is a need?

Well, maybe one day you see
that your neighbor's windows are really dirty
and that they really *need* to be cleaned.

Maybe you tell your neighbor
that you will clean his dirty windows
for a dollar and maybe he says, OK!

Wow! Now you are your own boss!
You thought of a need,
your neighbor's dirty windows,
and when you clean his dirty windows
he becomes your customer
and he pays you the dollar he promised!

Now, what if you find
a lot of dirty windows to clean…?

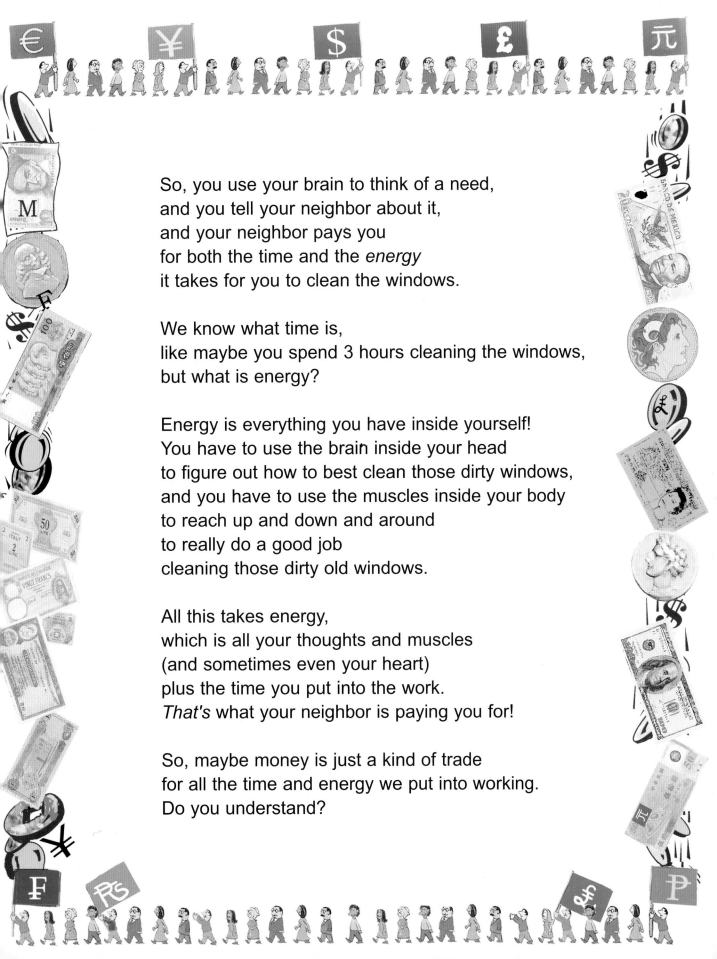

So, you use your brain to think of a need,
and you tell your neighbor about it,
and your neighbor pays you
for both the time and the *energy*
it takes for you to clean the windows.

We know what time is,
like maybe you spend 3 hours cleaning the windows,
but what is energy?

Energy is everything you have inside yourself!
You have to use the brain inside your head
to figure out how to best clean those dirty windows,
and you have to use the muscles inside your body
to reach up and down and around
to really do a good job
cleaning those dirty old windows.

All this takes energy,
which is all your thoughts and muscles
(and sometimes even your heart)
plus the time you put into the work.
That's what your neighbor is paying you for!

So, maybe money is just a kind of trade
for all the time and energy we put into working.
Do you understand?

What happens if your Mom or Dad gets sick
and they don't have enough energy to work
in order to pay for the stuff your family needs?

What if an earthquake happens, or a big storm,
and part of your house gets knocked down
and some of your clothes and stuff get ruined?

If somebody is too sick to work,
or if some bad stuff happens,
and a family needs money to fix things up,
sometimes they have to *borrow* money.

To borrow money means to ask somebody
to *lend* you some of their money.
When somebody lends you their money,
you have to promise to pay their money back
and you have to promise
to pay it back on a certain day.

Sometimes a friend,
or an aunt or an uncle, can lend you money.
Sometimes a *bank* can lend you money.
(A bank is a place where people keep the money
that they earn and can't hide under the mattress.)

But whoever lends you money,
you have to pay that money back
and on time, understand?

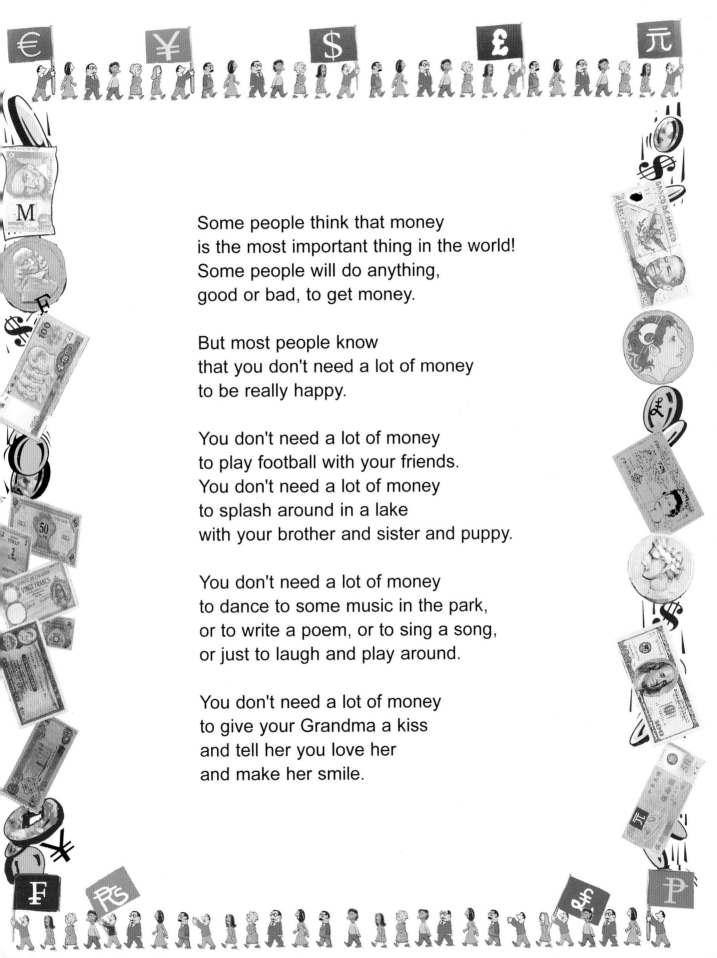

Some people think that money
is the most important thing in the world!
Some people will do anything,
good or bad, to get money.

But most people know
that you don't need a lot of money
to be really happy.

You don't need a lot of money
to play football with your friends.
You don't need a lot of money
to splash around in a lake
with your brother and sister and puppy.

You don't need a lot of money
to dance to some music in the park,
or to write a poem, or to sing a song,
or just to laugh and play around.

You don't need a lot of money
to give your Grandma a kiss
and tell her you love her
and make her smile.

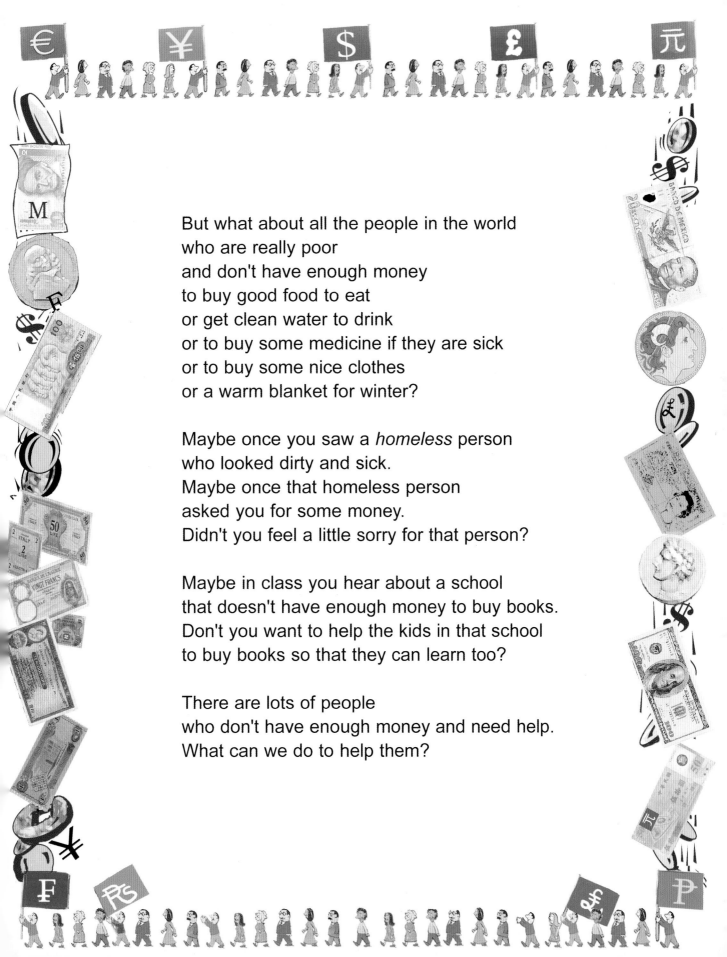

But what about all the people in the world
who are really poor
and don't have enough money
to buy good food to eat
or get clean water to drink
or to buy some medicine if they are sick
or to buy some nice clothes
or a warm blanket for winter?

Maybe once you saw a *homeless* person
who looked dirty and sick.
Maybe once that homeless person
asked you for some money.
Didn't you feel a little sorry for that person?

Maybe in class you hear about a school
that doesn't have enough money to buy books.
Don't you want to help the kids in that school
to buy books so that they can learn too?

There are lots of people
who don't have enough money and need help.
What can we do to help them?

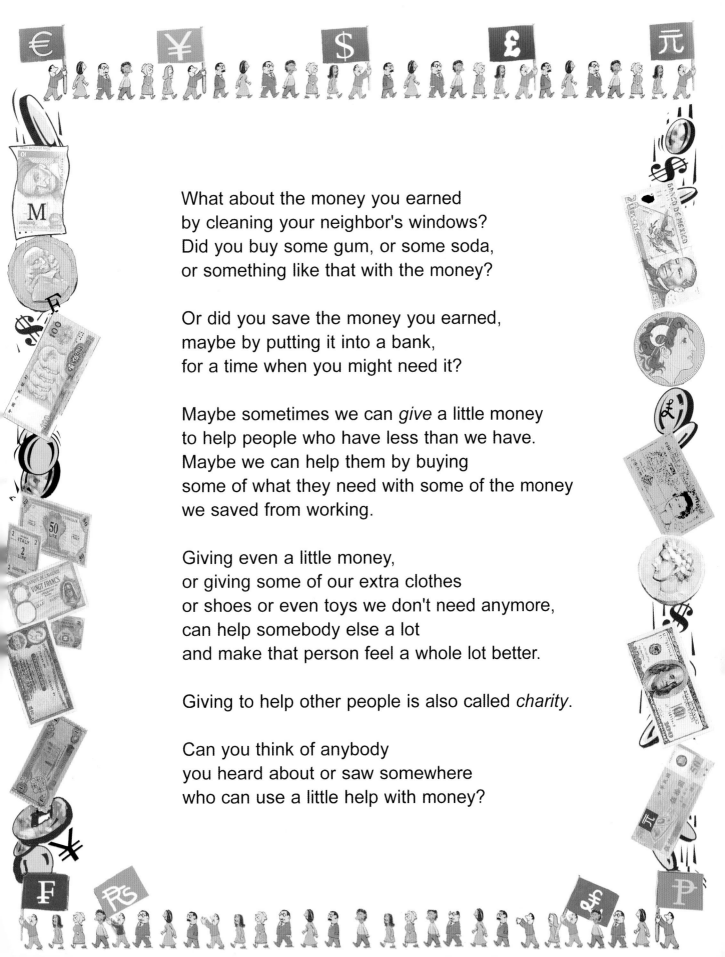

What about the money you earned
by cleaning your neighbor's windows?
Did you buy some gum, or some soda,
or something like that with the money?

Or did you save the money you earned,
maybe by putting it into a bank,
for a time when you might need it?

Maybe sometimes we can *give* a little money
to help people who have less than we have.
Maybe we can help them by buying
some of what they need with some of the money
we saved from working.

Giving even a little money,
or giving some of our extra clothes
or shoes or even toys we don't need anymore,
can help somebody else a lot
and make that person feel a whole lot better.

Giving to help other people is also called *charity*.

Can you think of anybody
you heard about or saw somewhere
who can use a little help with money?

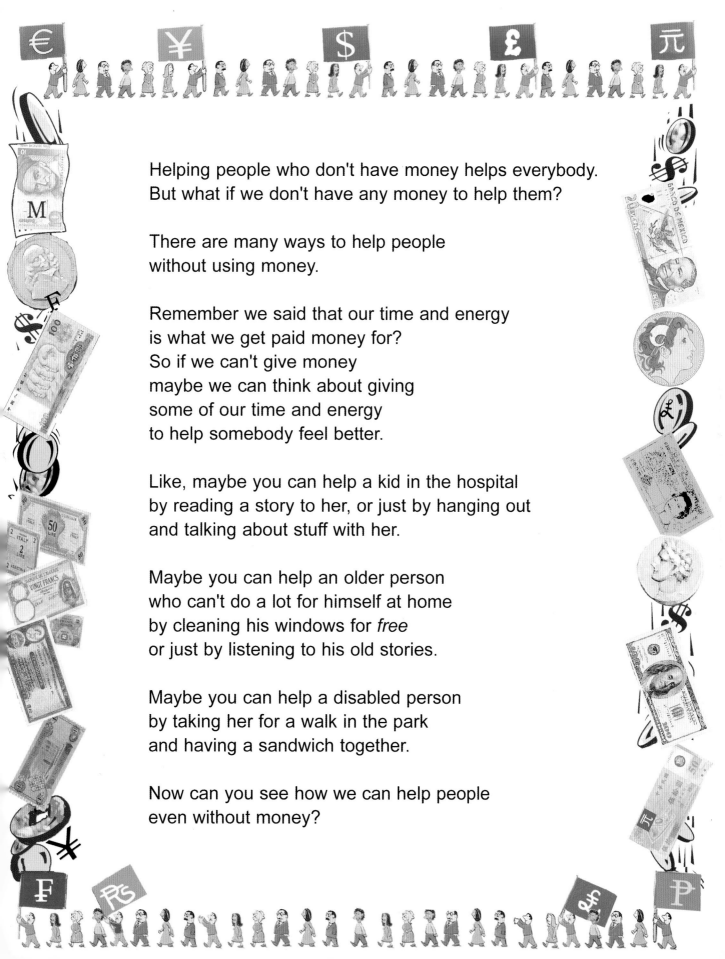

Helping people who don't have money helps everybody.
But what if we don't have any money to help them?

There are many ways to help people
without using money.

Remember we said that our time and energy
is what we get paid money for?
So if we can't give money
maybe we can think about giving
some of our time and energy
to help somebody feel better.

Like, maybe you can help a kid in the hospital
by reading a story to her, or just by hanging out
and talking about stuff with her.

Maybe you can help an older person
who can't do a lot for himself at home
by cleaning his windows for *free*
or just by listening to his old stories.

Maybe you can help a disabled person
by taking her for a walk in the park
and having a sandwich together.

Now can you see how we can help people
even without money?

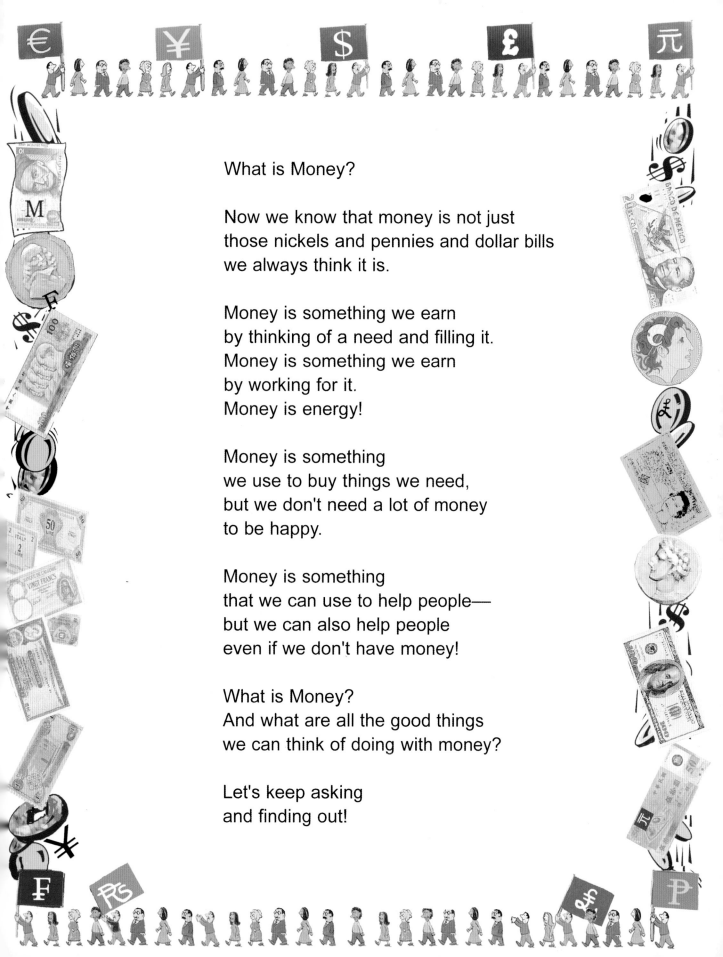

What is Money?

Now we know that money is not just
those nickels and pennies and dollar bills
we always think it is.

Money is something we earn
by thinking of a need and filling it.
Money is something we earn
by working for it.
Money is energy!

Money is something
we use to buy things we need,
but we don't need a lot of money
to be happy.

Money is something
that we can use to help people—
but we can also help people
even if we don't have money!

What is Money?
And what are all the good things
we can think of doing with money?

Let's keep asking
and finding out!